Natural Law

The Moral Foundation for Social and Political Civility

Jefrey D. Breshears

Areopagus Publishing

Areopagus Publishing
www.TheAreopagus.org

"Natural Law: The Moral Foundation for Social and Political
Civility"
By Breshears, Jefrey D.

ISBN: 978-0-9830680-2-0

*Special thanks to Randall Hough for providing the
initial inspiration and critical analysis for this booklet.*

Natural Law:
The Moral Foundation for
Social and Political Civility

*We have now sunk to a depth at which
re-statement of the obvious is the first duty
of intelligent men.* – George Orwell

The America of the past is fading fast. A culture war that was simmering mostly beneath the surface for generations has erupted in the past several decades into a raging conflict that pits starkly contrasting (and often irreconcilable) worldviews, ideologies, and value systems against one another. The effects of the culture war are apparent as our society and institutions are becoming increasingly polarized and dysfunctional – which is why our political leaders seem so incapable of handling even the most obvious problems. There is political gridlock in Washington, D.C. because there is moral and cultural gridlock in American society in general. The result – to cite the title of a Bob Dylan song from several years back – is that "Everything Is Broken."

The erosion of basic standards of honor and decency in our society today is truly alarming, and it is affecting every area of our culture from law and politics to business, education, the media, the judicial system, the arts and entertainment, public behavior, and private morality. In the process, the very character and nature of America is being radically transformed.

For cultural liberals, much of this change is cause for celebration. In their mind, the America of the past was characterized mainly by capitalistic exploitation, environmental spoilation, social injustice, sexual repression, racism, sexism,

1

xenophobia, homophobia, Christian hegemony, and global imperialism. Their remedy is to fundamentally change America in keeping with a more "progressive" agenda – an integral part of which is to relativize traditional morality while absolutizing their own version of ethics and "social justice" (by which they usually mean redistributing wealth). And although this is essentially a secular/socialist crusade, many Christians are actively promoting (or at least passively accommodating) this radical agenda.

Cultural conservatives, while acknowledging America's many flaws and failures, nonetheless believe (in varying degrees) in the concept of American exceptionalism. They hold that America has often functioned as a "city upon a hill" and a lighthouse to the nations. As a result, it became the most free, productive and prosperous nation the world has ever seen. Furthermore, it has often (but certainly not always) promoted the cause of freedom, justice, and humanitarianism around the world more than any other nation ever has. So for cultural conservatives – including perhaps most Christians – the secularization of America is troubling. In fact, it is one of the great tragedies in human history.

Some Christians, based on a superficial understanding of history and Christian social philosophy, call for a return to a "Christian America" that they imagine existed in the past. For them, the only solution to the moral and cultural disintegration we see all around us is the imposition of some kind of Christian theocracy based on the legal codes of Old Testament (i.e., pre-Christian) Israel. There is no question that America has been *uniquely influenced* by the Christian faith, but America has never been a "Christian nation" in any real sense of the term. (In fact, although there have been many nominally-Christian nations in history, there has never been – and will never be – one that is truly Christian.) The concept of a "Christian America" is not only bad history – it is blasphemous and one of the worst forms of idolatry.

That being the case, is there any common ground between social conservatives and liberals when it comes to accepting a baseline for morality, ethics, and civility? In fact there is, and it derives from a universal truth that was generally accepted until recent times – the concept of Natural Law.

What Is Natural Law?

As the term is used in philosophy, theology and the social sciences, Natural Law* does not relate to the natural physical laws that govern the material universe. Nor is it synonymous with the common law traditions on which the legal codes of various nations are derived. Rather, Natural Law constitutes the moral and ethical precepts that human beings sense intuitively as a result of being made in the *imago Dei* – the image of God.

In essence, Natural Law is a kind of moral-based common sense – a set of moral and ethical principles that is universal and transcultural, and that can be summarized in one simple concept: "Do good and avoid evil." In the history of philosophy the concept of Natural Law has sometimes been called the **"perennial philosophy,"** and in his writings **C. S. Lewis** often referred to it as the *Tao* (i.e., "the Way"), and explained its significance:

> This thing which I have called for convenience the *Tao*, and which others may call Natural Law or Traditional Morality or the First Principles of Practical Reason,... is not one among a series of possible systems of value. It is the sole source of all value judgements. If it is rejected, all value is rejected. [C. S. Lewis, *The Abolition of Man* (HarperSan Francisco, 1944, 1974), p. 43.]

As Christians have conceptualized Natural Law, these precepts are expressions of absolute and eternal norms, and are derived from God's **general revelation** in nature rather than his

* I have capitalized 'Natural Law' in this essay for the purpose of emphasis.

special revelation set forth in Scripture. General revelation relates to the evidence of God's character that is apparent to all humanity, being manifest in three ways: (1)in the creation of the physical world [Psalm 19:1-4; Acts 14:14-17; 17:24-28; Rom. 1:18-32]; (2)through God's providential sustenance and maintenance of his creation [Psalm 104]; and (3)in the reality of the human moral conscience [Gen. 1:26-27; Rom. 1:18-32; 2:14-15]. It is in relation to this third aspect of general revelation that Natural Law operates.

Being universal in scope, the moral and ethical precepts of Natural Law have been acknowledged, either explicitly or implicitly, by most all civilized societies throughout most of history. As William Gairdner emphasizes in *The Book of Absolutes*, these principles are not invented by human beings but simply discovered.

> We exist and discover a universe that is governed by natural physical laws, as we are. But in addition to our physical being, we humans have a unique higher consciousness and reasoning capacity that enable us to reflect on the meaning of existence and to discover the nature of the laws both governing the material world... and guiding human action.... Because all normal humans have a mind, they also have the capacity to reason rightly or wrongly and hence the moral freedom to choose for good or for evil. With this reason and moral freedom, humans everywhere and at all times have discovered a set of general natural laws or principles that they rely upon instinctively to guide individual and social existence....
>
> As a consequence of their common human nature and social existence we can see that all normal human beings carry the compass of natural law within; an innate sense concerning things like justice, fairness, equity, cheating, lying, love, courage, wisdom, and so on....
>
> Natural law provides a transcendent standard by which to judge not only our own behavior and that of others, but also to judge the behavior of governments

and states.... Natural law is always a quest for absolute values, justice and truth....

The whole structure of natural law forms an argument rooted in interlocking and persuasively self-evident principles and truths. [William D. Gairdner, *The Book of Absolutes: A Critique of Relativism and a Defence of Universals* (McGill-Queen's University Press, 20008), pp. 192-93; 182; 185.]

These "interlocking and persuasively self-evident principles and truths" are what the Christian philosopher J. Budziszewski refers to as "what we can't not know" – i.e., commonsensical precepts are so obvious that one has to intentionally deny their reality. [See Table A on page 6 for some key principles of Natural Law.]

However, although the basic precepts of Natural Law are universal, the *understanding* and *application* of them vary from one society to another. As with individuals, no two cultures are equal; some have higher standards or are more consistent in enforcing these principles than others. Of course, due to human sin, these principles are regularly ignored and violated for various reasons by those who have the power and the will to do so. Therefore, people choose to lie, cheat, steal, exploit and abuse others all the time for their own benefit. Nonetheless, we know intuitively that such acts are wrong for the simple reason that none of us wants to be the object or the victim of such behavior.*

---

* See the Appendix for the basic philosophical presuppositions underlying the Natural Law.

Table A
Some Basic Principles of Natural Law

- There is a God (or gods, or "First Cause," or some unifying power or principle) that is responsible for the existence and maintenance of the universe.
- There is a moral law to which we are accountable.
  - Certain attitudes, speech and actions are objectively right and wrong regardless of our personal/subjective feelings about them.
- The sanctity of human life and a prohibition on murder.
- The rule of law (either a formal written code or informal customs).
- The right of self-defense and protection from physical and/or emotional abuse by others.
- Private property rights.
- Protection from arbitrary government abuse or coercion.
- The promotion of virtues such as wisdom, honor, courage, and moderation.
- Honesty in normal interpersonal relations and commercial transactions.
- Standards of social decency and propriety.
- Sexual restrictions: The sanctity of marriage, and prohibitions on sexual promiscuity, incest and rape.
- Respect for one's parents, ancestors and elders.
- Proper protection and provision for children.
- The value of kindness, compassion, mercy, and forgiveness.
- The primacy of the common good over individual rights.
- The principle of reciprocity, and a tacit acknowledgment of the Golden Rule: "Do unto others as you would have them do unto you."
- The summary principle: "Do good and avoid evil."

Philosophical Origins of Natural Law

In recorded history, the concept of Natural Law can be traced back to the great philosophers of classical Greece: Socrates, Plato and Aristotle. Unlike the sophists, the pop philosophers of their day, **Socrates**, **Plato** and **Aristotle** were moralists who argued against skepticism, subjectivism, relativism, and individualism. In other words, they believed that truth was real, objective, absolute, and universal. They also believed in objective standards of goodness and justice.

Of the three, Aristotle wrote most extensively on Natural Law theory, and he had the most influence on later Christian thinkers

on this subject. In *Rhetoric* he distinguished between "nature" and "natural justice" (which he considered synonymous with goodness and virtue) and man-made laws, customs and traditions, which he acknowledged as imperfect. For Aristotle, civic laws should not only express absolute principles but also help shape character – i.e., make men virtuous. (Note: Aristotle defined virtue primarily as responsible citizenship that contributes to the common good of the *polis*, the Greek city-state.) Without an understanding of the biblical doctrine of the Fall, he nonetheless understood that virtue was not innate – it must be inculcated through moral-based education, socialization, and law. And while he recognized that true morality involves more than just good public behavior, he was convinced that we acquire virtue by doing the right thing consistently until it becomes habitual. So although men are not born virtuous, they can be trained to be virtuous. But all of this requires that civic laws mirror universal principles, and he contrasted this ideal of natural justice with the legal codes of the various Greek *poli* and found them all deficient in various ways.

Over the next several centuries Greek and Roman Stoic philosophers continued to develop the idea that there are moral and ethical precepts that are absolute and immutable. For Stoics, the key to living virtuously was to order one's life in accord with Nature, commonly expressed in the concept of the *Logos* – the divinely-ordained unifying principle of Reason that governs the universe.

It was Roman jurists who first coined the term "Natural Law" (*Ius Naturale*). As applied to legal theory, the concept incorporated certain basic human rights that governments should acknowledge, codify, honor and protect. In his work on political philosophy, *The Republic*, **Cicero** (106-43 BC) declared that true justice is rooted in divinely-established universal principles. He wrote that "true law is right reason consonant with nature, diffused among all men, constant and eternal" – the purpose of which is to provide for "the safety of citizens... and the tranquility and happiness of human life." Influenced by his Stoic predecessors, Cicero repudiated

the popular skepticism, relativism and sophistry of his day and acknowledged God as the author and enforcer of the moral law. He noted that legitimate laws reward virtue, discourage vice, and promote the common good, while unjust laws are illegitimate because they violate Reason and the natural order of the universe.

The Apostle Paul on Natural Law

In his Epistle to the Romans, the apostle **Paul** alludes to the concept of Natural Law and contends that it is written on the human heart. This law, he infers, transcends manmade laws and is accessible by human reason because it is innate and intuitive. Human beings who transgress the moral law do so knowingly and intentionally, not out of ignorance. Therefore, they are morally accountable before God and without excuse.

Rom. 1:18*ff* – For the wrath of God is being revealed from heaven against all the godlessness and wickedness of men who suppress the truth by their wickedness, since what may be known about God is plain to them, because God has made it plain to them.

For since the creation of the world God's invisible qualities – his eternal power and divine nature – have been clearly seen, being understood from what has been made, so that men are without excuse.

For although they knew God, they neither glorified him as God nor gave thanks to him, but their thinking became futile and their foolish hearts were darkened. Although they claimed to be wise, they became fools and exchanged the glory of the immortal God for [idols and] images....

Therefore God gave them over in the sinful desires of their hearts to sexual impurity for the degrading of their bodies.... They exchanged the truth of God for a lie, and worshiped and served created things rather than the Creator.... Furthermore, since they did not think it worthwhile to retain the knowledge of God, he gave them over to a depraved mind....

They have become filled with every kind of wickedness, evil, greed and depravity. They are full of envy, murder, strife, deceit and malice. They are gossips, slanderers, God-haters, insolent, arrogant and boastful, they invent ways of doing evil; they disobey their parents; they are senseless, faithless, heartless, ruthless. Although they know God's righteous decree that those who do such things deserve death, they not only continued to do these very things but also approve of those who practice them.

Rom. 2:14ff – Indeed, when Gentiles, who do not have the [Mosaic] law, do by nature things required by the law, they are a law for themselves, even though they do not have the law, since they show that the requirements of the law are written on their hearts, their consciences also bearing witness, and their thoughts now accusing, now even defending them.

According to Paul, the value of this innate moral law is that it convicts us of sin and our need for divine redemption. But the moral law cannot save us from the consequences of sin. Spiritual salvation comes only through God's grace by way of our faith in the atoning death of Jesus Christ, not through moral living or acts of sacrifice on our part. So while the moral law is valuable in terms of convicting us of our need for salvation, it is impotent in and of itself in terms of providing that salvation that we so desperately need.

Interestingly, the most prominent Stoic philosopher of the first century AD, Seneca (4 BC - 65 AD), affirmed much of what Paul wrote about Natural Law. Unlike the polytheistic pagans of his day, Seneca believed in a good and just monotheistic God who governed the universe. Although clearly not a Christian, he was highly regarded by some Christians who believed he had been influenced by Paul during his time in Rome. Without any apparent understanding of Christian theology, Seneca contended that every individual has an innate sense of God-consciousness, and that God was both transcendent and immanent:

> God is near you, he is with you, he is within you. This is what I mean... a holy spirit indwells within us, one who marks our good and bad deeds, and is our guardian.... No man can be good without the help of God.

The Early Development of Natural Law

Some early Church Fathers, most notably **Augustine of Hippo** (354-430), incorporated the concept of Natural Law into their moral philosophy. Then in the 6th century the Byzantine emperor **Justinian II** (r. 527-65) appointed a commission of scholars under the renowned jurist Trebonian to gather and classify the disorganized mass of law that had accumulated over 800 years of Roman rule. The resultant **Code of Justinian**, a monumental achievement in legal codification, functioned as the basis for most European legal codes for the next thousand years. The *Institutes*, an introductory volume to the Justinian Code, defined "natural laws" as those that are "established by divine providence and always remain firm and immutable." A century later **Isidore of Seville** (c. 560-636) composed his encyclopedic *Etymologies* in which he identified Natural Law as both the foundation and the standard for the moral law common to all nations.

In the 12th century the canon lawyer **Gratian** compiled an anthology of ecclesiastical laws, the *Decretum*, in which he analyzed the various types of laws that regulated human behavior. Gratian acknowledged Natural Law as the root of all morality, noting that "The human race is ruled by two things, namely, natural law and legal customs," and he declared the very essence of Natural Law to be the Golden Rule – "to do to others what one would want done to himself" [Matt. 7:12].

Thomas Aquinas on Natural Law

The traditional Christian understanding of Natural Law was refined and transmitted to the modern world primarily through the writings of **Thomas Aquinas** (1225-74), a renowned philosopher/theologian and the most influential thinker of the

entire medieval era. Influenced by Aristotle (whom he referred to as "*the* Philosopher"), Aquinas argued in his *magnum opus*, **Summa Theologica**, that it is possible to know certain things about God and morality based on God' general revelation in nature, quite apart from his special revelation in Scripture. In other words, the natural mind, even without special divine insight, can arrive at general truths about God and morality through the natural world and human reason

because they are self-evident. So in effect, general revelation establishes a kind of common ground between Christians and non-Christians that can be used as a point of contact in Christian apologetics and evangelism.

Being made in the *imago Dei*, we have the moral law in our hearts by virtue of our human nature which corresponds to divine truth revealed in Scripture. All truth is God's truth, whether accessed by theology or philosophy. Both faith and reason come from God, and God cannot by his very nature contradict himself. However, general revelation can take us only so far. The comprehension of deeper and more specific moral and spiritual truths – including specific aspects of the character of God and his purpose for our life – requires special revelation.

For Aquinas, the starting point for moral theology is the doctrine of law. The origin of every just law is the **Eternal Law**, which is an expression of the character and nature of God, the Supreme Judge of the universe – or as Aquinas explains it, think of God as the sun and the Eternal Law as the sunlight. Derivative of the Eternal Law is **Natural Law**, those foundational principles of universal morality that govern human interactions. As the apostle Paul emphasized in Romans 1, Natural Law is written in the hearts of all men, its precepts are self-evident, and it is binding on all humanity.

According to Aquinas, the primary goal of Natural Law is to direct humanity toward the Good – i.e., ultimately toward God. Therefore, the Natural Law is not sufficient in itself and must be complemented by the **Divine Law**, which is the manifestation of Eternal Law revealed explicitly in Scripture. Finally, the culmination of Divine Law is the **New Covenant**, the Gospel of Jesus Christ, which is fulfilled in the **Law of Love** as encapsulated in the Golden Rule and the Greatest Commandment [Matt. 7:12; 22:37-40].

So in Thomistic moral philosophy, Natural Law is indispensable in terms of being the gateway to the garden of the Gospel, which is activated when, by divine grace, we love the Lord God with all our heart, soul, mind and strength, and love our neighbor as our self.

Regarding the relationship between Natural Law and manmade legal codes, Aquinas was adamant that the latter should conform to the former. In other words, all human laws are accountable to Natural Law, and any human law that contradicts Natural Law is unjust, illegitimate and indefensible. But beyond the recognition and implementation of Natural Law for the common public good, government has no right to impose higher-level Divine Law upon society in general. That would be counterproductive, as Divine Law is applicable only to those who voluntarily submit to the authority of God in their lives.

Protestantism and Natural Law

Natural Law remained the prevailing theory of jurisprudence until modern times despite the fact that during the Reformation the doctrine was somewhat controversial due to the Protestants' emphasis on Original Sin and *sola gracia* (salvation by grace alone). In his voluminous writings **John Calvin** scarcely mentioned Natural Law at all, although he added a terse reference to it in the final chapter of the *Institutes* in the context of Divine Law: "It is a fact that the [moral] law of God... is nothing less than a testimony of the natural law and of that conscience which God has engraved upon the minds of men."

Martin Luther was more expansive, describing Natural Law as a kind of "living book" that is written on the human heart.

There is no one who does not feel the natural law. Everyone must acknowledge that what it says is right and true.... If men would only pay attention to it, they would have no need of books or any other law. For they carry along with them in the depth of their hearts a living book which could give their quite adequate instruction about what they ought to do and not to do, how they ought to judge, and what ought to be accepted and rejected....

Experience itself shows that all nations share this common ordinary knowledge.... I feel in my heart that I certainly ought to do these things for God, not because of what traditional written laws say, but because I brought these laws with me when I came into the world.... For although the decalogue was given in one way at a single time and place, all nations recognize that there are sins and iniquities. [Quoted in J. Budziszewski, *Written on the Heart: The Case for Natural Law* (IVP Academic, 1997), p. 207*ff.*]

As a systematic theologian Luther was far more concerned with God's special revelation in Scripture than with the general revelation found in nature. So like Aquinas, he emphasized the limitations of the Natural Law and noted that due to the noetic effects of the Fall, "The devil so blinds and possesses hearts that they do not always feel this law." Nonetheless, he believed the church must "preach the law and impress it on the minds of people till God assists and enlightens them" to the point that they develop an acute awareness and sensitivity to sin. Yet, were the moral law "not naturally written in the heart," the human conscience would have no sense of God-consciousness and be virtually oblivious to the reality of right and wrong.

A generation after Luther and Calvin, the precepts of Natural Law theory figured prominently in the works of the Anglican theologian **Richard Hooker** (1554-1600) and the jurist **Sir Edward Coke** (1552-1634). Then most significantly, **William Blackstone** (1723-80), the preeminent legal scholar of the 18th century, built his entire philosophy of common law on the foundation of these principles. Blackstone considered the precepts of Natural Law to be  universal and timeless, and he contended that all valid laws "derive all their force and all their authority... from this original."

Not everyone was in accord. Some Protestant theologians took the "rejectionist" position that human reason and passions had been so utterly corrupted by the Fall as to render meaningless any concept of an innate moral consciousness. This was, in part, a reaction against traditional Thomistic Catholic theology, but like modern presuppositional apologists and many contemporary evangelicals, they cited verses such as Jeremiah 17:9 – "The heart is deceitful above all things, and desperately wicked" – to conclude that fallen man is not only spiritually dead but morally clueless.

For entirely different reasons, radical secularists such as **Thomas Hobbes** (c. 1588-1679) also sought to discredit the concept of Natural Law due to their preference for moral relativism. Nonetheless, the basic concept of Natural Law remained a generally accepted intellectual presupposition of Western Civilization until the 20th century.

The Enlightenment Revision

In America, the concept of Natural Law exerted a significant influence on colonial life and values. But with the dawn of the Enlightenment (the so-called "Age of Reason") a more humanistic version of Natural Law began to emerge in conjunction with the new theology of **deism**. At first virtually undetectable, there was a subtle shift in the underlying philosophy of Natural Law from a moral code deducible from natural theology to one that emanated from human reason alone.

As popularized particularly by the English political philosopher **John Locke** (1632-1704), this new orientation redirected the ultimate objective of Natural Law from the traditional goal of the *commonweal* (the common good) to one focused on individual rights, which Locke regarded as God-given, "inalienable," and coterminous with virtue. Like the economist Adam Smith would later assert, Locke assumed that as  reasonable civic-minded citizens pursued their own agenda, an "invisible hand" of sorts would guide and transform their actions to the benefit of society in general. Although a libertarian, Locke was no libertine. He understood that good government required an enlightened, a "religious," and a moral citizenry, and he regarded libertinism as irresponsible, immature, and harmful to the civic order. So although mistaken for a selfish pursuit, the striving for individual liberty works ironically to strengthen rather than weaken the social fabric.

By the time of the American Revolution this new interpretation of Natural Law, with its emphasis on inalienable individual rights, was becoming the jurisprudential "common sense" of the day. It was also an integral part of the whole socio/political ideology of **Classical Liberalism** upon which the American nation was founded.

Although originally subtle, the differences in traditional Natural Law and the Enlightenment revisionist view became increasingly apparent over time. In *The Book of Absolutes*, William Gairdner highlights many of these distinctions as summarized in Table B on page 17.

Lockean and deistic influences are evident in the **Declaration of Independence**. **Thomas Jefferson** later commented that the Declaration was simply "an expression of the American mind" at the time of the Revolution – or in other words, it reflected the common sense political thinking of the American people. Jefferson also claimed that the document was an original creation and that he "turned to neither book nor pamphlet while writing the Declaration." But in fact Locke's influence, including many specific arguments that he presented in his *Second Treatise on Government,* permeated Jefferson's writings (whether consciously or not). Among these Lockean and deistic influences are the aforementioned "unalienable rights" that derive from "the laws of nature and nature's God."

> When in the course of human events, it becomes necessary for one people to dissolve the political bands which have connected them with another, and to assume among the powers of the earth the separate and equal station to which the laws of nature and

Table B
Traditional Natural Law and Enlightenment Natural Rights

	Traditional Natural Law	Enlightenment Natural Rights
The Authority	Divine will and human reason.	Human will and reason.
Accessible via	Human nature – as a result of the *imago Dei*.	Legal codes and charters.
Basis of law	Eternal, absolute, universal.	Created by human reason and subject to change.
Epistemic basis	Intuition ("written on the heart")	Written in legal codes and charters.
Main theorists	Aristotle, Augustine, Aquinas.	Locke, Rousseau, Jefferson.
Human law	Should conform to absolute moral principles.	Should conform to the will of the people.
Main objective	The common good.	Individual freedom and happiness.
Human nature	Corrupt and must be regulated by absolute moral principles.	Good by nature, but corrupted by bad social systems.
Civil society	A good society is a moral society regulated by universal moral principles.	A good society is a free society that promotes individual autonomy.
Liberty	Liberty must be balanced by responsibility based on universal moral principles.	Morality is a private matter based on personal values.
Origin of evil	Internal – based on the rejection of moral absolutes.	External – based on unjust socio/political systems.
Political system	Should reflect the realities of the moral law and human nature.	Should reflect the will of the people.

Source: William D. Gairdner, *The Book of Absolutes: A Critique of Relativism* (McGill-Queen's University Press, 2008).

nature's God entitle them, a decent respect for the opinions of mankind requires that they should declare the causes which impel them to the separation.

We hold these truths to be self-evident, that all men are created equal, that they are endowed by their Creator with certain unalienable rights, that among these are Life, Liberty, and the Pursuit of Happiness. That to secure these rights, governments are instituted among men, deriving their just powers from the consent of the governed.

American patriots effectively exploited this revised version of Natural Law to generate support for independence from Great Britain. Had they adhered to the traditional understanding of the concept – let alone traditional Just War Theory* or the clear prohibitions in the New Testament against political rebellion – they could never have justified the Revolution.

The Emergence of Legal Positivism

Although a revised theory of Natural Law based primarily on individual rights continued to be taught in most American law schools into the 20th century, it was inadequate in terms of resisting the new intellectual currents of the day. Beginning in the mid-1800s, relativism, materialism and secularism – as popularized by Darwin, Marx, Freud, William James and others – launched a withering series of assaults on the premises of objective Truth in general and Christianity in particular.

Having disconnected Natural Law from its traditional moral framework derived from natural theology, some legal theorists began arguing for an alternative theory known as **Legal Positivism** (or "**Positive Law**"). Casting aside the belief that law should be founded on moral absolutes, Legal Positivists advocated a more pragmatic, utilitarian and relativistic theory of jurisprudence derived from social customs, common law,

---

* For an analysis of the correlation between Natural Law and Just War Theory, please see the Appendix.

statutory and case law, and judicial precedent. This constituted a radical shift in the underlying philosophy of Western jurisprudence, and the moral and ethical consequences of Legal Positivism over the past century have been truly catastrophic.

According to the tenets of Legal Positivism, laws are manmade, not divinely-sanctioned, and should reflect the will of the majority in keeping with democratic ideals. In the 19th century the foremost apostles of Legal Positivism were the English philosophers **Jeremy Bentham** (1748-1852) and **John Stuart Mill** (1806-73), and in American legal history this concept was promoted most notably by the U.S. Supreme Court Justice **Oliver Wendell Holmes Jr.** (served1902-32). Holmes was an energetic proponent of judicial relativism and a vocal opponent of Natural Law theory whose judicial philosophy is best encapsulated in his statement, "The life of the law has not been logic; it has been experience." In other words: there is no such thing as objective justice; there are only subjective interests and conflicts of interest. Therefore, jurisprudence is not guided by absolute principles applied by reason, but rather by subjective criteria derived from our social interactions and personal life experiences.

Holmes' philosophy set a dangerous precedent. If there are no moral absolutes – and if law is whatever the political and judicial elites (or the democratic majority) deem it to be – then even the most immoral laws can be rationalized. Historically, this has been a fundamental presupposition of tyrants from Julius Caesar to Saddam Hussein. All would agree that might makes right and that law is the legal exercise of raw power.

By the turn of the 20th century Legal Positivism was becoming the dominant jurisprudential philosophy in many elite law schools, and for more than a century this theory has been a major driving force in America's culture war. Although rarely acknowledged (other than by legal philosophers), it has provided the legal cover for the kind of philosophical relativism and judicial activism promoted by organizations such as the **American Civil Liberties Union (ACLU)**. By the 1940s the theory of "positive law" was entrenched in many American law schools to the extent that traditional Natural Law was commonly dismissed as a curious relic of the past.

But truth cannot be suppressed permanently, and since the 1980s there has been a revival of interest in Natural Law. In 1991 the controversy surfaced publicly during the Supreme Court confirmation hearings for **Clarence Thomas**, and it was a primary factor in the liberal attempt to defeat his nomination. (Unfortunately, this was obscured by the media's fixation on the sensationalistic and unsubstantiated allegations of sexual misconduct lodged against Thomas by a former law clerk, Anita Hill.) In his early writings Thomas had often cited Natural Law as a guiding principle in his judicial decisions. However, due in part to the Senate's previous rejection of another conservative nominee to the Court, **Robert Bork**, Thomas was prudently circumspect in openly discussing his philosophy of jurisprudence. Wisely, he limited his comments to a brief statement in which he affirmed his belief in Natural Law as "a philosophical background to the Constitution." Liberals were appalled, but Thomas' comments made many aware for the first time of the controversy over Natural Law theory that had been raging in juridical philosophical circles for a hundred years.

Natural Law and Martin Luther King Jr.'s "Letter from a Birmingham Jail"

Martin Luther King Jr. often appealed to Natural Law to justify non-violent social protest during the Civil Rights movement of the 1950s and '60s. Most notably, he penned his famous "Letter from a Birmingham Jail" following his arrest for organizing unauthorized street demonstrations in Birmingham, Alabama in 1963. In response to his critics – in particular, local white ministers who condemned him for advocating law-breaking – King defended his actions on the basis of traditional Christian moral philosophy. In the following excerpt from his eloquent and erudite essay, he cites Augustine and Aquinas and draws a clear distinction between just and unjust laws derived from the precepts of Natural Law.

You express a great deal of anxiety over our willingness to break laws. This is certainly a legitimate concern. Since we so diligently urge people to obey the Supreme Court's decision of 1954 outlawing segregation in the public schools, it may seem rather paradoxical for us consciously to break laws.

One may well ask: 'How can you advocate breaking some laws and obeying others?' The answer lies in the fact that there are two types of laws: just and unjust. I would be the first to advocate obeying just laws. One has not only a legal but a moral responsibility to obey just laws. Conversely, one has a moral responsibility to disobey unjust laws. I would agree with St. Augustine that "an unjust law is no law at all."

Now, what is the difference between the two? How does one determine whether a law is just or unjust? A just law is a man-made code that squares with the moral law or the law of God. An unjust law is a code that is out of harmony with the moral law. To put it in the terms of St. Thomas Aquinas: An unjust law is a human law that is not rooted in eternal law and natural law. Any law that uplifts human personality is just. Any law that degrades human personality is unjust. All segregation statutes are unjust because segregation distorts the soul and damages the personality. It gives the segregator a false sense of superiority and the segregated a false sense of inferiority.

Natural Law and Contemporary American Culture

Ours is a culture in crisis. We see all around us the consequences of a society that has forsaken not only Christian morality and ethics but even the most elementary principles of common sense, decency and civility. This is apparent to everyone except the most morally clueless (who, unfortunately, are often the most powerful and influential figures in our political, legal, educational, entertainment, and media institutions). Ideas have consequences, and the primary philosophical error underlying this breakdown is the rejection of absolute morality derived from the principles of Natural Law and the widespread (and mindless) acceptance of relativism in all its manifestations:

- Epistemological relativism declares that there is no truth – everything is a matter of perspective – and that nothing can be known for certain;
- Moral relativism rejects the idea of moral absolutes and asserts that nothing is necessarily right or wrong;
- Religious relativism (a.k.a. "religious pluralism") proclaims that no religion is universally or exclusively true and that all religious paths lead to God;
- Cultural relativism presumes that morality varies from one culture to another and that all are equally valid;
- Legal relativism (i.e., "Positive Law") posits that subjective psychological and sociological factors, in addition to extenuating circumstances, should influence legal decisions

rather than strict adherence to the rule of law;

- Historical relativism maintains that historical "truth" is purely subjective and dependent upon the particular values and points-of-view of historians themselves; and
- Aesthetic relativism holds that there are no objective standards for art, literature or music, and that one person's opinion is just as valid as another's.

These relativistic assumptions, although sometimes subtle, are absolutely insidious. As the Christian philosopher Peter Kreeft has noted, "Of all the symptoms of decay in our decadent civilization, relativism is the most disastrous of all." Similarly, Michael Novak warns of the cultural consequences of relativism:

Relativism is an invisible gas, odorless, deadly, that is now polluting every free society on earth. It is a gas that attacks the central nervous system of moral striving. The most perilous threat to the free society today is, therefore, not political nor economic. It is the poisonous, corrupting culture of relativism. [Michael Novak, "Awakening from Nihilism: The Templeton Prize Address." First Things (No. 45, Aug/Sep), p. 20.]

The antidote for relativism is Natural Law, which establishes a foundation for morals and ethics based on self-evident and common sensical truths that are essential to the normal functioning and maintenance of any civil society and its institutions. The precepts of Natural Law are also the foundation for global civility and international law. Despite vast differences between nations in terms of their histories, languages, races, traditions, customs, and social, economic and political systems, state leaders recognize that there are certain fundamental moral and ethical principles that underlie all international negotiations and agreements. Although seldom acknowledged publicly, this is a tacit concession to the fact that there is a moral law that transcends and precedes international law itself.*

* For an extended treatment of Natural Law as it relates to international law, see William Gairdner, The Book of Absolutes (cited earlier), and John Finnis, Natural Law and Natural Right (Clarendon, 1980).

Obviously, all societies would be better if they were regulated by Biblical principles – in which case there would be comparatively little corruption, injustice, exploitation, violence, etc. But mainstream society is not Christian, and as Christians we cannot and should not attempt to institute some kind of Christian theocracy or impose specifically Christian values on nonbelievers. To do so, we would need to utilize the coercive power of the state to force compliance, which would be not only futile but generally counterproductive. It would also violate the spirit of the Gospel.

The best that can be expected of any free society is a general recognition of the basic precepts of Natural Law and an honest attempt to promote and, when efficacious, enforce them. Anything else – whether it relates to Christian sexual morality, Biblical principles of social justice, or any other explicitly Christian values and behavior – should be proclaimed and practiced by the community of Christ but cannot and should not be forced on others. Church history is littered with sincere but ill-fated attempts to impose Biblical standards of morality on society-at-large, and these efforts have rarely accomplished anything other than to bring reproach on the Christian faith and provide fodder for our enemies.

Realistically, we must be content to simply heed the words of Christ: "You are the salt of the earth... [and] the light of the world. A city on a hill cannot be hidden.... In the same way, let your light shine so that others may see your good deeds and honor your Father in heaven" [Matt. 5:13*ff*]. Any attempts to go above and beyond the parameters of Natural Law impose standards of behavior that people who lack the internal guidance and power of the Holy Spirit cannot possibly meet. And even worse, any such attempts render the church of Jesus Christ a force for coercion and oppression rather than light and liberation.

A culture based on Natural Law would be one that insists upon an elementary level of common decency and civility conducive to the flourishing of both individual civil liberties and the general welfare of society as a whole. It would be a social and political environment dedicated to cultivating harmony, fairness, equal opportunity, true social justice, and the rule of law for everyone. While it wouldn't be utopia – no human society will ever approach perfection – it would be considerably more wholesome and healthy than our present society and culture. And most significantly, it would be fertile ground on which to freely sow and cultivate the seed of the Gospel of Jesus Christ.

◘

Jefrey Breshears, Ph.D., is a Christian historian, apologist, and the founder and president of The Areopagus, a Christian education ministry and study center in the Atlanta area that offers seminars and forums in Christian history, apologetics, Christian spirituality, and contemporary cultural issues.

JBreshears@TheAreopagus.org

Notes and Reflections

....
....
....
....
....
....
....
....
....
....
....
....
....
....
....
....
....
....
....
....
....
....

Questions for Reflection and Discussion

1. What is the thesis (the main point) of this essay?
2. Which point in this essay affected you the most, and why?
3. What are some areas in which you've noticed the effects of America's moral decline in recent years, and how have these changes affected you personally?
4. Why is the "Christian America" thesis an erroneous and counterproductive concept?
5. Give a short working definition of Natural Law.
6. Do all of the principles of Natural Law in Table 'A' strike you as being self-evident and universal? If not, which one(s) do you find questionable, and why?
7. By comparison to Roman Catholic philosophers and theologians, why do you think that many Protestants have been relatively tepid in their endorsement of Natural Law theory?
8. A criticism of traditional Natural Law theory is that it focused too much on the *commonweal*, whereas Enlightenment Natural Rights emphasized individual rights. How should Christians evaluate this tension, and what is the solution?
9. What about Table 'B' do you find most striking (or alarming), and why?
10. What are some recent examples of the influence of Legal Positivism in our legislative and judicial systems?
11. What most impresses you about Martin Luther King Jr.'s "Letter from a Birmingham Jail?"
12. How would a return to an understanding of Natural Law impact our society and culture – in particular, the media, popular culture, and our educational, political, economic and legal systems?

For Further Reading...

C. S. Lewis, *The Abolition of Man* (HarperSanFranciso, 1944).

Jacques Maritain, *The Rights of Man and Natural Law* (Gordian Press, 1971).

Jacques Maritain and William Sweet, *Natural Law: Reflections on Theory and Practice* (St. Augustine Press, 2001).

J. Budziszewski, *Written on the Heart: The Case for Natural Law* (IVP Academic, 1997).

J. Budziszewski, *The Line Through the Heart: Natural Law as Fact and Theory* (Intercollegiate Studies Institute, 2009).

Robert P. George, *In Defense of Natural Law* (Oxford University Press, 2001).

Robert P. George, *Clash of Orthodoxies: Law, Religion & Morality in Crisis* (Intercollegiate Studies Institute, 2002).

William Gairdner, *The Book of Absolutes: A Critique of Relativism and a Defence of Universals* (McGill-Queen's University Press, 2008).

Appendix

Natural Law and Just War Theory
Jefrey D. Breshears

Since the parameters of Natural Law cover the entire range of human relations, one would naturally assume that there are universal ethical principles that apply even in the moral morass that of warfare. Indeed there are, and the belief that it is permissible for Christians to participate in war under certain conditions was first articulated by **Augustine of Hippo** (354-430) in the early 400s. According to him, wars are sometimes necessary in order to deter a greater evil but should be conducted with maximum restraint according to specific guidelines.

Despite the difficulty in reconciling Just War theory with New Testament principles, the Roman Catholic Church officially sanctioned the concept. According to the teachings of the Church, Christian knights were holy warriors who had a moral responsibility to defend the Church, the poor, and the defenseless from aggressors. In the 850s **Pope Leo IV** (r. 847-55) promised heavenly rewards to anyone who died in battle defending the Church, and his successor, **Pope Nicholas I** (r. 858-67), declared that even those under a sentence of excommunication could bear arms for the Church if they did so against infidels. Several years later **Pope John VIII** (r. 872-82) proclaimed those who fought and died for the Church to be martyrs for Christ.

The first popular book that attempted to set ethical standards for Christian knights was *The Life of the Christian* (c. 1095), written by **Bishop Bonizo of Sutri** just prior to the First Crusade. In the 13th century, in an attempt to make war more humane, **Thomas Aquinas** (1225-74) sought to further refine the basic precepts underlying Just War theory. Throughout the Middle Ages the following principles established the proper rules for waging war.

(1)A defensive war.
- A just war is a defensive war only.
- One may fight only to protect one's self, dependents, and property.
- One should never provoke a conflict or engage in an offensive war of aggression.

(2)A limited war.
- Fighting must be restricted to combatants only.
- Clergymen, monks, and unarmed civilians must not be harmed.

(3)The sanctity of church property.
- Church buildings must not be damaged or looted.

(4)No fighting on holy days.
- No fighting and killing on feast days and Sundays.

(5)The principle of reciprocity.
- In waging a defensive war, the methods and goals should not exceed what is necessary to deter an act of aggression.

(6)The main objective.
- The main objective is to subdue one's enemy and halt his aggression – not to slaughter indiscriminately or plunder and destroy.

(7)A code of chivalry.
- When fighting fellow-aristocrats, knights should follow strict rules of conduct.
- It is improper to ambush an unarmed knight; any honorable knight should give his foe a chance to put on his armor before being attacked. (Armor was heavy and hot, and knights usually didn't wear it on hot days. Yet a knight never knew when he might be attacked, so this rule allowed him to travel in comfort with his armor loaded on a pack-horse.)
- Knights should treat their captives as guests – no torture or humiliation, and fellow-aristocrats should not be bound in chains and thrown into dungeons.

- Prisoners who promise a ransom should be set free so they can honor their agreement, and those who fail to raise the ransom should return voluntarily to captivity.

[Note: The rules of chivalry did not apply when waging crusades. Infidels and heretics were enemies of God, and no mercy was accorded them.]

In modern times Just War theory has been incorporated into international law and canonized as an authoritative doctrine of the Roman Catholic Church, confirmed by the United States Catholic Bishops in a 1983 pastoral letter, *The Challenge of Peace: God's Promise and Our Response*. In addition, the *Catechism of the Catholic Church* lists four conditions for "legitimate defense by military force:"

- The damage inflicted by the aggressor must be sufficiently serious;
- All other means of putting an end to the conflict must have been shown to be impractical or ineffective;
- There must be realistic prospects for success; and
- The use of arms must not produce "evils and disorders" greater than the evil being eliminated.

Simply stated, most contemporary Just War theoreticians would agree with Augustine that war, though always regrettable, is sometimes necessary in order to deter a greater evil, but it must be fought with humanitarian restraint and the intention of establishing a just and lasting peace. War is permissible if it is defensive in nature or if it liberates innocent people from excessive tyranny on the part of an oppressive government that violates their right to life, liberty or property.

As currently conceptualized, three criteria define a Just War:

(1)Just Cause (*Jus ad bellum*).

- The reason for going to war must be just.
- Innocent life must be in imminent danger, and the purpose for intervention must be to protect life. In 1993 the United States Catholic Conference stated, "Force may be used only to correct a grave, public evil, i.e., aggression or massive violation of the basic human rights of whole populations."
- Nations have a right to self-defense against other nations that would violate their national sovereignty.
- Only a duly constituted government may wage war – not rebel factions intent on spawning a revolution.
- War cannot be waged in order to conquer territory or gain control over another nation's human or material resources.
- There must be a "probability of success" – i.e., war must not be waged in a futile cause .
- The principle of "last resort:" Force may be employed only after all peaceful and viable alternatives have been seriously attmpted and exhausted.

(2)Just Force (*Jus in bello*).

- Once a war has begun, it must be fought in accordance with Just War principles.
- The principle of distinction: War must be directed toward enemy combatants, not civilians. Innocent civilians must not be killed, terrorized or molested, nor their property destroyed unnecessarily.
- The principle of proportionality: A minimum amount of force should be employed that is necessary to deter aggression or stop the oppression of a people by a tyrannical government.
- Prisoners of war should be treated humanely.

(3)Just Peace (*Jus post bellum*).
- Defeated aggressors should acknowledge their guilt, offer compensation to their victims, and submit to war crimes trials in the interest of full justice.
- Guilty parties are subject to just punishment for their crimes against humanity in accord with the principle of proportionality.
- Revenge on the part of victors is prohibited, including the exploitation of the human and material resources of the defeated nation(s).

Just as these Just War principles have been generally acknowledged in theory, they have been regularly violated in practice. In fact, Just War theory has always been more of an ideal than a reality, and once an armed conflict begins the rules of engagement are often quickly ignored. Nonetheless, like the Ten Commandments or any other moral code, the principles of Just War are useful and, undoubtedly, have had some tempering affect on the violence and inhumanity perpetrated in at least some wars. And for that we should be duly grateful.

◘

Notes and Reflections

....
....
....
....
....
....
....
....
....
....
....
....
....
....
....
....
....
....
....
....
....
....
....
....
....

Philosophical Presuppositions of Natural Law

by *Randall J. Hough*

The truth of Natural Law theory arises out of an understanding of the truth of some basic philosophical principles. Correspondingly, the recognition of these philosophical principles derives from reflection upon the nature of sensible reality.

The theory of Natural Law presupposes the existence of certain truths which, when understood, help explain the nature of the universe in general as well as particular aspects of its content. But to understand these truths, one must acknowledge that the very concepts of existence, nature, laws, knowing, and understanding are not themselves physical but metaphysical in essence. They are philosophical constructs of the human mind discovered through normal cognition and right reason.

It follows, then, that to grasp the truths of Natural Law one should be familiar with its philosophical presuppositions – both as they relate to the nature of being (ontology) and the nature of knowing (epistemology). The following table, derived in part from William Gairdner's *Book of Absolutes: A Critique of Relativism and a Defence of Universals* (McGill-Queen's University Press, 2008), summarizes the essential philosophical presuppositions of Natural Law.

Philosophical Presuppositions of Natural Law

- All natural objects operate according to regular principles.
- These principles themselves are not physical but metaphysical (or philosophical).
- Humans, unique among natural life forms, can discover and understand these philosophical principles by experience and reason.
- All living things change and grow toward their natural ends according to their distinctive natures. (Acorns become oak trees, caterpillars become butterflies, fetuses become human beings, etc.)
- Humans also have natural ends which include not only our physical makeup (babies become adults) but also our rational makeup.
- These rational ends include personal virtue, human interactions (including family), and human flourishing within communities.
- The principles that govern human development of personal virtue, human interactions, and human communities comprise the content of Natural Law.
- As rational beings, humans must deliberately act in accordance with the principles of Natural Law to bring about these rational ends.
- Humans are unique in that we have the capacity to comprehend the correlation between cause and effect and calculate the consequences of our actions.
- The foregoing gives rise to the most basic principle of Natural Law: Seek that which is good and avoid that which is evil.

(continued)

Philosophical Presuppositions of Natural Law
(continued)

- Deliberately acting in accordance with the principles of Natural Law is good and leads to human flourishing, while deliberately acting against these principles is evil and leads away from human flourishing.
- Certain moral values derive from Natural Law such as wisdom, justice, fairness, honesty, courage, moderation, modesty, self-defense, the sanctity of the family, and property rights.
- Derivative of these values is the realization of the priority of the common good over individual autonomy and the acknowledgment that might does not make right.
- All of these values indicate an intuitive grasp of the universal Natural Law as a standard of justice higher than human law.
- Implicit in Natural Law is the priority of goodness and justice over personal wants, which constitutes the basis for the understanding that natural moral laws exist as transcendent principles.
- The state is guided by, and subject to, the same moral and ethical principles of Natural Law as individuals in the pursuit of the common good.
- Human laws, whether enacted by individuals, legislators, judges, or by executive fiat, are innately unjustifiable if they abrogate the principles of the Natural Law.

Randall Hough is an associate director of The Areopagus and a trustee of Southern Evangelical Seminary in Charlotte, N.C.

Notes and Reflections

....

....

....

....

....

....

....

....

....

....

....

....

....

....

....

....

....

....

....

....

....

....

....

....

....

Made in the USA
Charleston, SC
07 September 2013